United States Government Accountability Office

I0410922

Testimony

Before the Subcommittee on Oversight, Committee on Ways and Means, House of Representatives

For Release on Delivery
Expected at 10:30 a.m. ET
Wednesday, July 23, 2014

PATIENT PROTECTION AND AFFORDABLE CARE ACT

Preliminary Results of Undercover Testing of Enrollment Controls for Health Care Coverage and Consumer Subsidies Provided Under the Act

Statement of Seto J. Bagdoyan, Acting Director, Forensic Audits and Investigative Service

GAO-14-705T

July 2014

GAO Highlights

Highlights of GAO-14-705T, a testimony before the Subcommittee on Oversight, Committee on Ways and Means, House of Representatives

PATIENT PROTECTION AND AFFORDABLE CARE ACT

Preliminary Results of Undercover Testing of Enrollment Controls for Health Care Coverage and Consumer Subsidies Provided Under the Act

Why GAO Did This Study

PPACA provides for the establishment of health insurance exchanges, or marketplaces, where consumers can compare and select private health insurance plans. The act also expands the availability of subsidized health care coverage. The Congressional Budget Office estimates the net federal cost of coverage provisions at $36 billion for fiscal year 2014, with subsidies and related spending accounting for a large portion. PPACA requires marketplaces to verify application information to determine enrollment eligibility and, if applicable, eligibility for subsidies.

GAO was asked to examine issues related to controls for application and enrollment for coverage through the federal marketplace. This testimony discusses preliminary observations on (1) results of undercover testing in which we obtained health care coverage; (2) additional undercover testing, in which we sought to obtain consumer assistance with our applications; and (3) delays in the development of a system needed to analyze enrollment.

This statement is based on preliminary analysis from GAO's ongoing review for this subcommittee and other congressional requesters. GAO created fictitious identities to make applications through the federally facilitated exchange in several states by telephone, online, and in-person. The number and locations of the target areas are not disclosed because of ongoing testing. The results, while illustrative, cannot be generalized to the overall applicant or enrollment populations. GAO expects to issue a final report next year.

View GAO-14-705T. For more information, contact Seto Bagdoyan at (202) 512-6722 or BagdoyanS@gao.gov.

What GAO Found

Centers for Medicare & Medicaid Services (CMS) officials told us they have internal controls for health care coverage eligibility determinations. GAO's undercover testing addressed processes for identity- and income-verification, with preliminary results revealing questions as follows:

- For 12 applicant scenarios, GAO tested "front-end" controls for verifying an applicant's identity or citizenship/immigration status. Marketplace applications require attestations that information provided is neither false nor untrue. In its applications, GAO also stated income at a level to qualify for income-based subsidies to offset premium costs and reduce cost sharing. For 11 of these 12 applications, which were made by phone and online using fictitious identities, GAO obtained subsidized coverage. For one application, the marketplace denied coverage because GAO's fictitious applicant did not provide a Social Security number as part of the test.

- The Patient Protection and Affordable Care Act (PPACA) requires the marketplace to provide eligibility while identified inconsistencies between information provided by the applicant and by government sources are being resolved through submission of supplementary documentation from the applicant. For its 11 approved applications, GAO was directed to submit supporting documents, such as proof of income or citizenship; but, GAO found the document submission and review process to be inconsistent among these applications. As of July 2014, GAO had received notification that portions of the fake documentation sent for two enrollees had been verified. According to CMS, its document processing contractor is not required to authenticate documentation; the contractor told us it does not seek to detect fraud and accepts documents as authentic unless there are obvious alterations. As of July 2014, GAO continues to receive subsidized coverage for the 11 applications, including 3 applications where GAO did not provide any requested supporting documents.

- For 6 applicant scenarios, GAO sought to test the extent to which, if any, in-person assisters would encourage applicants to misstate income in order to qualify for income-based subsidies. However, GAO was unable to obtain in-person assistance in 5 of the 6 initial undercover attempts. For example, one in-person assister initially said that he provides assistance only after people already have an application in progress. The in-person assister was not able to assist us because HealthCare.gov website was down and did not respond to follow-up phone calls. One in-person assister correctly advised the GAO undercover investigator that the stated income would not qualify for subsidy.

A key factor in analyzing enrollment is to identify approved applicants who put their policies in force by paying premiums. However, CMS officials stated that they do not yet have the electronic capability to identify such enrollees. As a result, CMS must rely on health insurance issuers to self-report enrollment data used to determine how much CMS owes the issuers for the income-based subsidies. Work is underway to implement such a system, according to CMS, but the agency does not have a timeline for completing and deploying it. GAO is continuing to look at these issues and will consider recommendations to address them.

_____ United States Government Accountability Office

Chairman Boustany, Ranking Member Lewis, and Members of the Subcommittee:

I am pleased to be here today to discuss enrollment for health care coverage under the Patient Protection and Affordable Care Act (PPACA).[1] Among other things, the act provides subsidies to those eligible to purchase private health insurance plans, and with those subsidies and other costs, represents a significant, long-term fiscal commitment for the federal government. According to the Congressional Budget Office, the estimated net cost of coverage provisions to the federal government are $36 billion for fiscal year 2014 and $1.4 trillion for fiscal years 2015–2024, with subsidies and related spending accounting for a large portion of the total.[2] Because subsidy costs arising from the act are contingent on who obtains coverage, enrollment controls that help ensure only qualified applicants are approved for coverage or subsidies are a key factor in determining federal expenditures under the act.

PPACA, signed into law on March 23, 2010, provides for the establishment of health insurance exchanges, or marketplaces, to assist consumers in comparing and selecting among insurance plans offered by participating private issuers of health care coverage.[3] These marketplaces were intended to provide a single point of access for individuals to enroll in private health plans, apply for income-based subsidies to offset the cost of these plans—which are paid directly to health insurance issuers—and, as applicable, obtain an eligibility determination for other health coverage programs, such as Medicaid or the State Children's Health Insurance Program. The Department of Health and Human Services' (HHS) Centers for Medicare & Medicaid

---

[1]Pub. L. No. 111-148, 124 Stat. 119 (Mar. 23, 2010), as amended by the Health Care and Education Reconciliation Act of 2010 (HCERA), Pub. L. No. 111-152, 124 Stat. 1029 (Mar. 30, 2010). In this testimony, references to PPACA include any amendments made by HCERA. Future citations to PPACA will identify the applicable section of law without providing a full citation, as set forth here.

[2]Net costs are gross costs, including items such as income-based subsidies, minus revenue produced, such as through penalties paid by employers and uninsured people. See Congressional Budget Office, *Updated Estimates of the Effects of the Insurance Coverage Provisions of the Affordable Care Act* (April 2014).

[3]Specifically, the act required, by January 1, 2014, the establishment of health insurance exchanges in all states. In states not electing to operate their own exchanges, the federal government was required to operate an exchange.

Services (CMS) is responsible for overseeing the establishment of these online marketplaces. CMS has worked with a variety of contractors to develop, test, and maintain the federally facilitated marketplace known to the public as HealthCare.gov. At the time we conducted the work described in this statement, CMS was operating HealthCare.gov, also known as the Health Insurance Marketplace (Marketplace), in 36 states.

To be eligible to enroll in a qualified health plan offered through a marketplace, an individual must be a U.S. citizen or national, or otherwise lawfully present in the United States; reside in the marketplace service area; and not be incarcerated (unless jailed while awaiting disposition of the charges). Marketplaces, in turn, are required by law to take several steps to verify application information to determine eligibility for enrollment and, if applicable, determine eligibility for the income-based subsidies.[4] These verification steps include validating an applicant's Social Security number, if one is provided;[5] verifying citizenship, status as a national, or lawful presence with the Social Security Administration (SSA) or the Department of Homeland Security; and verifying household income and family size against tax-return data from the Internal Revenue Service, as well as data on Social Security benefits from the SSA.[6]

My statement today is based on preliminary results and analysis from ongoing work we are conducting at the request of the subcommittee and others. Specifically, today's statement (1) assesses, by means of undercover testing in which we obtained health care coverage, the Marketplace application and enrollment processes, including opportunities for potential enrollment fraud, during the act's first open enrollment period, which ran from October 2013 to April 2014;[7] (2) describes additional undercover testing, in which we sought to obtain

---

[4]PPACA, § 1411(c), 124 Stat. at 226-227; 45 C.F.R. §§ 155.310, 155.315, 155.320.

[5]An exchange must require an applicant who has a Social Security number to provide the number. 45 C.F.R. § 155.310(a)(3)(i).

[6]For a fuller discussion of the act's provisions related to eligibility determinations for enrollment in coverage and related subsidies, see app. I.

[7]Fraud involves obtaining something of value through willful misrepresentation. Whether conduct is in fact fraudulent is a determination to be made through the judicial or other adjudicative system. See GAO, *Standards for Internal Control in the Federal Government, 2013 Exposure Draft*, GAO-13-830SP (Washington, D.C.: September 2013), 40.

consumer assistance with our applications; and (3) describes delays in the development of the system needed to analyze enrollment.

To perform our undercover testing of the Marketplace application and enrollment processes, we created 18 fictitious identities for the purpose of making applications for individual health care coverage by telephone, online, and in-person.[8] Because of the federal government's role in operating marketplaces in the 36 states, we targeted our work on the federal Marketplace. We selected several states within the federal Marketplace for our undercover applications, based on factors including population size, mixture of population living in rural versus urban areas, and number of people qualifying for income-based subsidies under the act. We further selected target areas within each state, based on factors including community size. Because our testing work is ongoing, we do not disclose here the number or locations of our target areas. We generally selected our states and target areas to reflect a range of characteristics. To maintain independence in our testing, we created our applicant scenarios without knowledge of specific control procedures that CMS or other federal agencies may use in accepting or processing applications. We thus did not create the scenarios with intent to focus on a particular control or procedure.[9] Because the number of fictitious applications we made was limited, and the applications do not reflect a sample of actual applications, the results of our testing, while illustrative, cannot be generalized to the overall applicant or enrollment population.

For 12 of the 18 applicant scenarios, we tested "front-end" controls for verifications related to the identity or citizenship/immigration status of the applicant.[10] We made half of these applications online and half by phone. In these tests, we also stated income at a level eligible to obtain both

---

[8]For all our applicant scenarios, we sought to act as an ordinary consumer would in attempting to make a successful application. For example, if, during online applications, we were directed to make phone calls to complete the process, we acted as instructed.

[9]We were aware of general eligibility requirements, however, from public sources such as websites.

[10]Among other things, these tests simulated "identity theft," where a person misuses the identity information of another. We distinguish between "front-end" controls, which are preventative in nature and seek to diminish the opportunity for fraudulent access into a system, and "back-end" controls, which occur after an applicant has entered a system. See GAO, *Individual Disaster Assistance Programs: Framework for Fraud Prevention, Detection, and Prosecution*, GAO-06-954T (Washington, D.C.: July 12, 2006).

types of income-based subsidies available under PPACA—a premium tax credit and cost-sharing reduction.[11] Our tests included fictitious applicants who provided invalid Social Security numbers, noncitizens claiming to be lawfully present in the United States, and applicants who did not provide Social Security numbers. As appropriate, in our applications for coverage and subsidies, we used publicly available information to construct our scenarios. We also used publicly available hardware, software, and materials to produce counterfeit documents, which we submitted, as appropriate for our testing, when instructed to do so. We then observed the outcomes of the document submissions, such as any approvals received or requests received to provide additional supporting documentation.

For the remaining 6 of our 18 applicant scenarios to examine enrollment in the Marketplace, we sought to test only income-verification controls. We randomly selected three "Navigator" and three non-Navigator in-person assisters in our target areas.[12] For half of these 6 applications, our applicant planned to state income slightly above the maximum amount allowable for income-based subsidies, while for the others, our applicant planned to state income slightly below the range eligible for these subsidies. We sought to test the extent to which, if at all, any of the in-person assisters would encourage applicants to misstate income in order to qualify for either of the individual PPACA subsidies.

For all three objectives, we also reviewed laws, regulations, and other policy and related information. In addition, we also interviewed CMS officials to obtain an understanding of the application data that CMS maintains and reports.

---

[11]To qualify for these income-based subsidies, an individual must be eligible to enroll in marketplace coverage; meet income requirements; and not be eligible for coverage under a qualifying plan or program, such as affordable employer-sponsored coverage, Medicaid, or the State Children's Health Insurance Program.

[12]CMS has awarded $67 million in grants for "Navigators," which are individuals or organizations that are to provide, without charge, impartial health insurance information to consumers, and to help consumers complete eligibility and enrollment forms. In addition, such aid is also to be available from other in-person assisters ("non-Navigators") who generally perform the same functions as Navigators, but are funded through separate grants or contracts. Navigators and non-Navigator assisters must complete comprehensive training, according to CMS. Through the HealthCare.gov website, CMS published a state-by-state list of where in-person assistance can be obtained.

We are conducting our performance audit in accordance with generally accepted government auditing standards. Those standards require that we plan and perform the audit to obtain sufficient, appropriate evidence to provide a reasonable basis for our findings and conclusions based on our audit objectives. We believe that the evidence obtained provides a reasonable basis for our findings and conclusions based on our audit objectives. We are conducting our related investigative work in accordance with investigative standards prescribed by the Council of the Inspectors General on Integrity and Efficiency.

We Obtained Coverage in 11 of 12 Applications Made through Undercover Testing

The federal Marketplace approved coverage for 11 of our 12 fictitious applicants who initially applied online, or by telephone.[13] We later received notices in 10 of 11 of these cases that failure to submit documentation needed to verify eligibility could lead to loss of coverage or subsidies we received.[14] For 1 of the 11 approvals, we initially were denied coverage, but were successful when we subsequently reattempted the application. Applicants for coverage are required to attest that they have not intentionally provided false or untrue information. Applicants who provide false information are subject to penalties under federal law, including fines and imprisonment.[15] For each of the approved applications, we were ultimately directed to submit supporting documentation to the Marketplace, such as proof of income, identity, or citizenship.

[13]In the one application in which we failed to obtain coverage, our fictitious phone applicant declined to provide what was a valid Social Security number, citing identity theft concerns.

[14]Where the marketplace identifies certain inconsistencies in an application that it cannot resolve through reasonable effort, the marketplace must undertake an "inconsistency process," under which the applicant is typically given 90 days to present satisfactory evidence to resolve the identified inconsistencies. During this time, the marketplace must allow the applicant to enroll in a qualified health plan, and, if applicable, receive premium tax credit and cost-sharing reduction subsidies.

[15]In addition to penalties under federal criminal law, PPACA imposes civil penalties up to $25,000 for failure to provide correct information due to negligence or disregard of applicable rules, and up to $250,000 for knowingly and willfully providing false or fraudulent information.

GAO-14-705T

Preliminary Results of Front-End Controls Testing

For each of our 11 approved applications, we paid the required premiums to put policies into force, and are continuing to pay the premiums. For the 11 applications that were approved for coverage, we obtained the advance premium tax credit in all cases.[16] The total amount of these credits for the 11 approved applications is about $2,500 monthly or about $30,000 annually. We also obtained cost-sharing reduction subsidies, according to Marketplace representatives, in at least 9 of the 11 cases.[17] As noted, these advance premium tax credits and cost-sharing reductions are not paid directly to enrolled consumers; instead, the federal government pays them to issuers on consumers' behalf. To receive advance payment of the premium tax credit, applicants agree that they will file a tax return for the benefit year, and applicants receiving premium tax credits during the inconsistency period must indicate their understanding that premium tax credits are subject to reconciliation on their federal tax return.[18]

For each of our 6 online applications that were among the total group of 12, we failed to clear an identity checking step during the front end of the

---

[16] Thus, as of July 2014, GAO continues to receive subsidized coverage for the 11 applications.

[17] Income requirements for the tax credits and cost-sharing reduction subsidies are as follows:

- Those earning from 100 percent to 400 percent of the federal poverty level (adjusted for family size) are eligible for premium tax credits. These are federal income-tax credits, which eligible enrollees may elect to have paid in advance to health insurance issuers to offset premium costs. The federal poverty level varies by location. For the 2013–2014 open enrollment period, for example, the federal poverty level for the 48 contiguous states and the District of Columbia ranged from income of $11,490 for a single-person household to $39,630 for a household of eight.

- Those earning from 100 percent to 250 percent of the federal poverty level are also eligible for cost-sharing reduction subsidies. This is a reduction in a policyholder's nonpremium costs of coverage, such as for deductibles or copayments for covered services.

The number of our applications receiving cost-sharing reduction subsidies is likely higher because we stated our income at a level to obtain these subsidies. Marketplace representatives to whom we spoke did not always state whether our applicant had qualified for this subsidy. In addition, because the value realized through the cost-sharing reduction subsidy varies according to medical services used, value for such subsidies can likewise vary.

[18] Cost-sharing reduction subsidies are not subject to reconciliation on the taxpayer's federal income-tax return.

online application process, and thus could not complete the process online.[19] However, we subsequently were able to obtain coverage for all 6 of these applications begun online by completing them by phone. In 5 of these 6 cases, the online system directed us to contact a Marketplace contractor that handles identity checking. The contractor was unable to resolve the identity issues. According to a CMS public information website, if the contractor cannot resolve the issue, applicants may be asked to provide identity documents, by online upload or by mail. In such cases, according to CMS officials, applications are to be put on hold until identity proofing is completed. For this group of 5 applications, however, contractor representatives did not ask us to submit identity documents but instead directed us to call the Marketplace. We did, and after speaking with Marketplace representatives as instructed, we were able to successfully proceed with our applications by phone and obtain coverage for the 5 applications. In the sixth case, the online system directed us to call the Marketplace directly, without contacting the contractor. In that case, too, we proceeded to successfully complete the application by phone and obtained coverage.[20] According to CMS officials and executives of the Marketplace's call center contractor, an identity discrepancy must be cleared and identity verified before an application can proceed to completion.

For our 6 phone applications, we successfully completed the application process, with the exception of one applicant who declined to provide a Social Security number and was not allowed to proceed.

In the course of follow-up dealings with the Marketplace, call-center representatives in at least four cases could not locate our existing applications and, as a result, began new applications, according to our

---

[19]For online applications, the Marketplace employs a process known as identity proofing to verify an applicant's identity. This is done by using personal and financial history on file with a credit reporting agency. The Marketplace generates questions, based on information on file, that only the applicant is believed likely to know. If an applicant's identity cannot be verified, applicants are directed to call a credit reporting agency that is CMS's contractor for completing the identity-proofing process, for assistance in completing the proofing process.

[20]We were unaware of what procedure, if any, the Marketplace representatives used in clearing our applications for completion and submission. Because we were on the phone with Marketplace representatives, we could not observe how our applications were handled, and the Marketplace representatives did not otherwise indicate on what basis the applications were allowed to continue.

conversations with the representatives. According to CMS call-center and document-processing contractors, multiple electronic applications have been common.

Preliminary Results of Back-End Controls Testing

The Marketplace is required to seek postapproval documentation in the case of certain application "inconsistencies"—instances in which information an applicant has provided does not match information contained in data sources that the Marketplace uses for eligibility verification at time of application, or such information is not available. If there is an application inconsistency, the Marketplace is to provide eligibility while the inconsistency is being resolved using "back-end" controls.[21] Under these controls, applicants will be asked to provide additional information or documentation for a Marketplace contractor to review in order to resolve the inconsistency.

Among the 11 of our 12 undercover applications that successfully obtained coverage, the Marketplace initially directed that we submit supplementary documentation in 10 cases, with a request for supplementary documentation in the 11th case coming a few months after approval of coverage. Among the Marketplace communications were the following:

- The Marketplace asked two of three applicants with inactive Social Security numbers to submit proof of citizenship, identity, and income, but it asked a third only for income information.
- In four cases, the Marketplace asked for additional documentation a few months after initial document requests were made.
- The Marketplace directed two applicants to log into online accounts for messages—but these applicants had no such online accounts.
- The Marketplace sent unclear reminders to three applicants to file supplementary documentation, with a cover letter directing applicants to submit one type of document to resolve a particular inconsistency (for example, income), but then in an enclosure to be returned to the Marketplace requesting that another type of document be sent (for example, citizenship).

As part of our testing and in response to Marketplace requests, we provided counterfeit follow-up documentation, but varied what we

---

[21]PPACA, §§ 1411(e)(3)-(4), 124 Stat. at 228-229; 45 C.F.R. § 155.315(f)(4).

submitted by application—providing all, none, or only some of the material requested—in order to note any differences in outcomes. Specifically, among the 10 applications for which we were directed to send documentation at the time of approval, we submitted

- all requested documentation for 3 of the 10 applications,
- partial documentation for 4 applications, and
- no documentation for the remaining 3 applications.[22]

In addition, in 2 cases in which we were directed to submit income information, we reported income substantially higher than the amount we initially stated on our applications, and at levels that should disqualify our applications from obtaining subsidies.

CMS officials told us that a CMS contractor evaluates follow-up documentation on a rolling basis as it receives submissions. If the contractor deems the information submitted to be complete, a decision on eligibility is typically made within 1 to 2 days, according to the officials.[23] Otherwise, applicants may be directed to submit additional information as deemed necessary. In all cases, CMS officials told us, applicants are to be notified of the outcome of the review of their submitted documentation.

For the seven applications for which we elected to submit full or partial follow-up documentation, approximately 3 months have elapsed since we submitted the requested information. As of July 17, 2014, we had received notifications indicating the Marketplace had reviewed portions of the counterfeit documentation sent for two applications. Specifically, the Marketplace notified both these applicants that their proof of citizenship/immigration status had been verified and no further action is

---

[22]As noted, any documentation we supplied was, like our initial applications, fictitious, having been fabricated using commercially available hardware, software, and materials.

[23]CMS officials referred to this process as "adjudication" of the filings.

necessary.[24] One of them also had identity verified. We are awaiting notice on other documents filed for these two applicants.[25]

In the time since we filed documents requested at time of approval, we have received a number of follow-up communications from the Marketplace, which, as noted earlier, include requests for documentation not originally requested. In response, we have submitted a second round of documents, which responds to the requests but also maintains our testing methodology of submitting all, none, or some of the items requested. As of July 17, 2014, outcomes were still pending for these applications. Regardless of the status of any postapproval communications, our coverage remains in effect for all 11 approved applications.

Overall, among all applications for the federal Marketplace, about 4.3 million application inconsistencies have been identified, representing about 3.5 million people, according to the CMS contractor handling receipt and evaluation of submitted materials. Of the total inconsistencies, about 2.6 million are for applicants who took the step of selecting health care plans after completing their applications. As of mid-July 2014, about 650,000 inconsistencies had been cleared. However, according to contractor executives, due to system limitations, processing of income and citizenship/immigration status inconsistencies—which together account for 75 percent of inconsistency volume—began in May and June

---

[24]For both applications, the Marketplace also sent additional letters following verification. In these letters, the Marketplace requested we send supporting documentation to clear the inconsistencies, unless we had already received notification that the inconsistencies had been cleared—which we had received. We called the Marketplace to inquire about these postverification letters. For both applications, the marketplace representatives advised us to resend the supporting documentation. In addition, for one application, the Marketplace representative stated a representative would call the applicant to provide an explanation for this issue. As of July 17, 2014, we had not received such a call from the Marketplace.

[25]We are awaiting notice on the other documents because according to the CMS contractor handling document submissions, supporting documents are processed individually, rather than being considered all together for a particular application.

2014.[26] In some cases, according to the CMS contractor, documents cannot be matched to their respective applications, and become "orphans." As of mid-July 2014, the contractor said, there had been about 227,000 such documents. According to the contractor executives, unmatched documents are retained and reconsidered every 21 days to see if new information is available that can enable a match to be made.

As noted, applicants attest at the time of application that information they provide is not false or untrue. According to CMS officials, its document processing contractor is not required under its contract to authenticate documentation or to conduct forensic analysis. Executives of the contractor concurred, and told us the review standard the contractor uses is that it accepts documents as authentic unless there are obvious alterations. According to the executives, the contractor does not certify authenticity, does not engage in fraud detection, and does not undertake investigative activities. Specifically, in the contractor's standard operating procedures for its work for CMS, document review workers are directed under "general verification guidance" to "determine if the document image is legible and appears unaltered by visually inspecting it." Further, the contractor is not equipped to attempt to identify fraud, the contractor executives told us, and the contractor does not have the means to judge whether documents submitted might be fraudulent. The standard of accepting authenticity unless there is obvious alteration originated from CMS, the executives said.

According to the contractor executives, when consumers send copies of documents, as directed, rather than originals, there inevitably is a loss of image quality such that the contractor could not closely examine whether a document is authentic.[27] Costs would increase by several times to thoroughly analyze document authenticity, the CMS contractor executives

---

[26]The HHS Office of Inspector General recently reported on applicant inconsistencies, noting that the Marketplace was unable to resolve a high fraction of inconsistencies because the CMS eligibility system was not fully operational. Noting that each applicant can have multiple inconsistencies, the report said that inconsistencies do not necessarily indicate an applicant provided inaccurate information or is enrolled in a plan or receiving subsidies inappropriately. The report also addresses inconsistency resolution among state-based exchanges. See Department of Health and Human Services, Office of Inspector General, *Marketplaces Faced Early Challenges Resolving Inconsistencies With Applicant Data*, OEI-01-14-00180 (Washington, D.C.: June 2014).

[27]Incoming documents are also scanned, which means copies are made of the copies submitted.

told us. Even if such an effort was attempted, they said, it would be difficult to say if anti-fraud measures would be effective, because that is not the company's business.

The contractor also does not currently make use of outside data sources in its document review; instead, it inspects what documents are received.[28] Overall, the contractor executives told us, the contractor is not aware of any fraudulent applications and that, based on its practices, it also is not in a position to know whether fraud is being attempted. CMS officials similarly told us they did not know the extent of any attempts at application or enrollment fraud, but said that to date, there is no evidence of applicants defrauding the federal Marketplace.

In following through on our applications, we also identified a potential challenge to consumers obtaining information about review of documentation submitted. In communications we received from the Marketplace about our document submissions, we were directed to call the Marketplace with questions. When we called to inquire about the status of our document filings, representatives could not answer our questions. They told us they were not able to confirm receipt of requested documentation and were not able to provide information on whether requested documentation has been reviewed. The CMS contractors handling consumer calls and document verification each confirmed to us that the call centers cannot access document-submission information. Hence, it is currently not possible for a call-center representative, fielding an inquiry such as ours, to obtain document status information in order to provide that information to the consumer.

Overall, CMS officials told us that they have internal controls for the eligibility-determination process, and that experience has not shown the need for any changes in that process. They said that thus far, the focus has been on stabilizing processes being implemented for the first time.

Our work continues on the postapproval verification process. In particular, we are tracking whether we receive any additional adjudication notices

---

[28]At the time of our review, contractor executives told us they were soon to begin accessing a U.S. Department of Homeland Security data system for the limited purpose of checking documents submitted that had expired during the review process. They said, however, this does not constitute "external verification" and instead is a means to access updated versions of documents already received.

from the CMS verification contractor, or whether the contractor identifies supporting documentation we submitted as fictitious or inconsistent with information submitted at time of application. We will continue to assess CMS's management of the application and approval process through our ongoing work and consider any recommendations needed to address these issues.[29]

We Were Unable to Obtain In-Person Assistance in Five of Six Undercover Attempts to Test Income-Verification Controls

We attempted six in-person applications, in order to test income-verification controls only. Specifically, we sought to determine the extent to which, if any, in-person assisters would encourage our applicants to misstate income in order to qualify for either of the income-based PPACA subsidies.[30] According to CMS, in-person assistance is to be available for those seeking assistance in filing applications.[31] For these six in-person applications, we randomly chose three Navigators and three non-Navigators in the target areas of our selected states. For the in-person applications, because our sole interest was any potential advice on reporting income, we did not seek or obtain policies, as we did with our phone and online applications.

During our testing, we visited one in-person assister and obtained information on whether our stated income would qualify for subsidy. In that case, a Navigator correctly told us that our income would not qualify for subsidy. However, for the remaining five in-person applications, we were unable to obtain such assistance. We encountered a variety of situations that prevented us from testing our planned scenarios, including the following:

---

[29]Our work in this area may not be complete for a number of months, given flexibility provided under the act for CMS to extend the postapproval verification period. PPACA, § 1411(e)(4), 124 Stat. at 228.

[30]In these in-person applications, our planned approach was not to lead the assisters toward encouraging applicants to misstate income, but instead, as applicable, to discuss concerns about policy costs and to inquire if there were ways to reduce the expenses.

[31]According to a CMS website: "No matter what state they live in, consumers are able to get live in-person help as they go through the process of applying for and choosing new coverage options in the Marketplace." See Centers for Medicare & Medicaid Services, *Assistance Roles to Help Consumers Apply & Enroll in Health Coverage Through the Marketplace*, CMS Product No. 11647-P (January 2014).

- One of the three Navigators required that we make an appointment in advance by phone. When we were unable to reach the Navigator by phone, we made an in-person visit. The Navigator declined to provide assistance, or to schedule an appointment, saying instead we would need to phone to schedule an appointment to return.
- One of the three non-Navigators initially said it provides assistance only after people already have an application in progress. The non-Navigator did offer to assist us with an application, but the HealthCare.gov website was down. He directed us to call later for assistance. After we did so, this non-Navigator did not respond to three follow-up phone calls.
- Another of the three non-Navigators, a health care services company, told us it only handles applications from those having a medical bill at its medical facility.
- The third non-Navigator did not provide assistance, telling us it handles only applications for Medicaid.

In two of the five instances in which we were unable to obtain assistance at our originally selected locations, we proceeded to seek assistance at other randomly selected locations in our target areas. In these follow-up attempts, we again encountered difficulty in obtaining assistance for our applicants, including the following:

- For one test, we visited two additional locations beyond the initial location before finding an in-person assister at a third who correctly told us our income was insufficient to qualify for subsidy. At the first two locations, we were told, among other things, that appointments were necessary.
- For another test, which occurred late in the open-enrollment period, non-Navigator representatives declined to provide help, telling us they were uncomfortable doing so and planned to take a seminar on enrollment.

We further pursued, by phone calls to the Marketplace, the applications for which we could not get explicit in-person guidance on income and qualification for subsidy. In these calls, we were correctly advised that our income was outside the range eligible for income-based subsidy.[32]

---

[32]We believe, however, that as an investigative technique, a telephone interaction is qualitatively different from an in-person interaction, the former of which offers less personal contact between the parties and more difficulty in developing rapport. For that reason, we originally designed our testing for in-person contact.

Figure 1 summarizes our process and results for each of the groups of applicants—the 12 phone and online applications, and the six in-person attempts.

Figure 1: Preliminary Results of GAO Undercover Testing of Patient Protection and Affordable Care Act (PPACA) Application Process

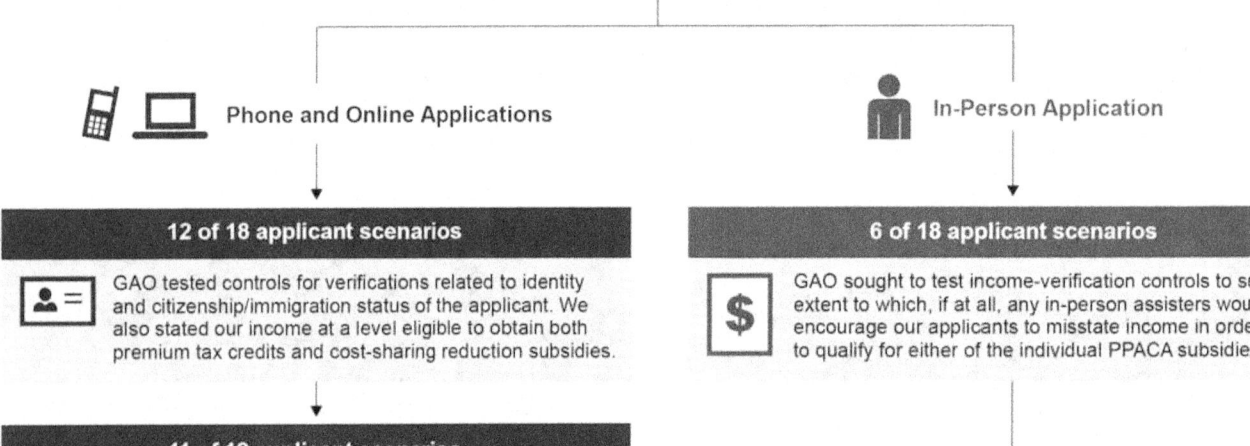

Undercover testing of Patient Protection and Affordable Care Act (PPACA) enrollment

↓

18 applicant scenarios
GAO created 18 fictitious identities for the purpose of making undercover applications for individual health coverage, by telephone, online, and in-person.

Phone and Online Applications

In-Person Application

12 of 18 applicant scenarios
 GAO tested controls for verifications related to identity and citizenship/immigration status of the applicant. We also stated our income at a level eligible to obtain both premium tax credits and cost-sharing reduction subsidies.

6 of 18 applicant scenarios
GAO sought to test income-verification controls to see the extent to which, if at all, any in-person assisters would encourage our applicants to misstate income in order to qualify for either of the individual PPACA subsidies.

11 of 12 applicant scenarios
GAO obtained coverage through the Health Insurance Marketplace (Marketplace).

For the 11 approved applications
 The Marketplace asked for supplementary documentation for all 11 approved applications—10 initially, and one a few months later. GAO later received notices in 10 of 11 of these cases that failure to submit documentation needed to verify eligibility could lead to loss of coverage or subsidies received.

1 of 6 applicant scenarios
 GAO was able to successfully visit one in-person assister and obtain information on whether our stated income would qualify for subsidy.

5 of 6 applicant scenarios
 GAO was unable to obtain assistance and encountered a variety of situations that prevented us from testing our planned scenarios.

Submission of documentation
GAO submitted fictitious documentation for all, none, or some documents requested for each approved applicant. Some fictitious documentation has been verified, as testing continues.

Source: GAO | GAO-14-705T

CMS Does Not Yet Have the Capability to Identify Those Who Have Paid for Policies, Limiting Our Ability to Analyze Enrollment

The federal government, in administering the two income-based subsidies, makes payments to issuers of health insurance on behalf of eligible consumers who have enrolled in a qualified health plan. According to CMS officials, individuals are considered to be enrolled in a plan after they pay the initial premium.[33] Thus, a key factor in analyzing enrollment in Marketplace coverage—and federal expenditures and subsidies that follow—is the ability to identify which applicants approved for coverage have subsequently paid premiums and put policies in force.

According to HHS, more than 8 million people selected a plan for coverage during the initial open-enrollment period that ended in April. CMS officials, however, told us they are thus far unable to identify individuals who have made premium payments. Issuers have reported this information to CMS, but the agency has not yet created a system to process the information, according to CMS officials.

In May 2014, CMS officials told us that work is underway to implement such a system. However, CMS does not have a timeline for completing and deploying this work. As a result, under current operations, CMS must rely on health insurance issuers to self-report enrollment data reflecting individuals for whom CMS owes the issuers the income-based subsidies arising from obtaining coverage through the Marketplace. We plan to continue examining this issue, among others, as part of our ongoing work, and to consider any recommendations needed to address it.

Chairman Boustany, Ranking Member Lewis, and Members of the subcommittee, this concludes my statement. I would be pleased to respond to any questions that you may have.

GAO Contact and Staff Acknowledgments

For questions about this statement, please contact Seto Bagdoyan at (202) 512-6722 or BagdoyanS@gao.gov. Contact points for our Offices of Congressional Relations and Public Affairs may be found on the last page of this statement.

---

[33]For subsidy-eligible individuals, this means payment of any portion of the premium not covered by the subsidies.

Individuals making key contributions to this statement include: Wayne A. McElrath, Director; Matthew Valenta, Gary Bianchi, and Kristi Peterson, Assistant Directors; Carrie Davidson; Paul Desaulniers; Sandra George; Robert Graves; Barbara Lewis; Maria McMullen; George Ogilvie; Shelley Rao; Ramon Rodriguez; Christopher H. Schmitt; Julie Spetz; Cherié Starck, Helina Wong; Elizabeth Wood; and Michael Zose.

Appendix I: Legal Appendix

This appendix provides background on certain requirements related to the submission of applications and eligibility-verification procedures to enroll in qualified health plans and qualify for income-based subsidies under the Patient Protection and Affordable Care Act (hereafter PPACA).[1]

To be eligible to enroll in a qualified health plan offered through a marketplace established under PPACA, an individual must be a U.S. citizen or national, or otherwise be lawfully present in the United States; reside in the marketplace service area; and not be incarcerated (unless pending disposition of the charges).[2] In addition, certain low- and moderate-income individuals and families may be eligible for income-based subsidies authorized by PPACA to make coverage more affordable: (1) a refundable tax credit, generally paid on an advance basis, to reduce premium costs for marketplace coverage (referred to as premium tax credits) and (2) reductions in cost-sharing associated with such coverage (known as cost-sharing reductions) for items such as copayments for physician visits or prescription drugs.[3] To qualify for either subsidy, an individual must meet applicable income requirements and must not be eligible for coverage under another qualifying plan or program, such as affordable employer-sponsored coverage, Medicaid, or the State Children's Health Insurance Program.[4] Subsidy payments are made to the issuer of the qualified health plan to offset the cost of the plan to the individual.[5]

Individuals seeking coverage under a qualified health plan offered through a marketplace may apply via the Internet, by telephone through a call center, by mail, or in person, using a single application that collects information necessary to determine enrollment eligibility and, if applicable,

---

[1]PPACA, Pub. L. No. 111-148, 124 Stat. 119 (Mar. 23, 2010), as amended by the Health Care and Education Reconciliation Act of 2010 (HCERA), Pub. L. No. 111-152, 124 Stat. 1029 (Mar. 30, 2010). In this appendix, references to PPACA include any amendments made by HCERA. Future citations to PPACA will identify the applicable section of law without providing a full citation, as set forth here.

[2]PPACA, § 1312(f)(1), (3),124 Stat. at 183-184; 45 C.F.R. § 155.305(a).

[3]PPACA, § 1401(a), 124 Stat. at 213-219 (adding 26 U.S.C. § 36B); id. at § 1402, 124 Stat. at 220-224.

[4]Id.; 45 C.F.R. § 155.305(f)-(g).

[5]PPACA, § 1412(c), 124 Stat. at 232-233.

subsidy eligibility.[6] Applicants for coverage are to attest that they have not intentionally provided false or untrue information. Applicants who provide false information are subject to penalties under federal law, including fines and imprisonment.[7]

Marketplaces are required by law to take several steps to verify application information to assess eligibility for enrollment in a qualified health plan and, if applicable, to qualify for an income-based subsidy. These verification steps include validating an applicant's Social Security number, if one is provided;[8] verifying an applicant's citizenship, status as a national, or lawful presence with the Social Security Administration (SSA) and/or the Department of Homeland Security; verifying household income and family size against the most recent tax-return data from the Internal Revenue Service (IRS), as well as data on Social Security benefits from the SSA; and verifying whether the applicant is eligible for health coverage under another qualifying plan or program that would preclude eligibility for subsidy purposes.[9]

Where the marketplace identifies certain inconsistencies in an application that it cannot resolve through reasonable effort, the marketplace must undertake an "inconsistency process," under which the applicant is given 90 days to present satisfactory evidence to resolve the identified

---

[6]45 C.F.R. § 155.405. An individual who applies via the Internet must first complete identity proofing, a step instituted by CMS to prevent someone from applying for health coverage without the named applicant's knowledge. According to CMS guidance, individuals who seek to apply for coverage through the federal Marketplace by submitting an online application and are unable to complete the electronic identity proofing process may be asked to submit satisfactory documentation of identity to the marketplace. CMS, *FAQ on Remote Identity Proofing, Remote Identity Proofing Failures and Application Inconsistencies (Federally-facilitated Marketplace)*, (May 21, 2014).

[7]In addition to any applicable penalties for perjury under federal criminal law, PPACA imposes civil penalties up to $25,000 for failure to provide correct information due to negligence or disregard of applicable rules, and up to $250,000 for knowingly and willfully providing false or fraudulent information. PPACA, § 1411(h)(1), 124 Stat. at 230. CMS recently issued a final rule, in which it specified how it intends to impose such penalties. Patient Protection and Affordable Care Act; Exchange and Insurance Market Standards for 2015 and Beyond. 79 Fed. Reg. 30,240, 30,290 (May 27, 2014) (to be codified at 45 C.F.R. § 155.285).

[8]An exchange must require an applicant who has a Social Security number to provide the number. 45 C.F.R. § 155.310(a)(3)(i).

[9]PPACA, § 1411(c), 124 Stat. at 226-227; 45 C.F.R. §§ 155.315(b)-(c), 155.320(b)-(c).

inconsistencies.[10] For example, the inconsistency process applies when the marketplace is unable to validate an individual's Social Security number or attestation regarding citizenship or immigration status.[11] It also applies when the marketplace is unable to verify eligibility for income-based subsidies, including, for example, if an applicant indicates a change in circumstances, such as substantial changes in income compared with the most recent tax return available, or IRS does not have recent tax-return data.[12] During the inconsistency period, the marketplace must allow the applicant to enroll in a qualified health plan and, if applicable, authorize the advance payment of any premium tax credit or cost-sharing reduction to the applicant's issuer on the basis of the applicant's attestations.[13]

In general, if a marketplace is unable to resolve the inconsistency after 90 days, it is required to determine eligibility based on the information contained in federal and other electronic data sources.[14] However, for applicants who do not have documentation to resolve an inconsistency (e.g., due to homelessness or natural disaster), a marketplace is required to provide an exception, on a case-by-case basis, to accept an applicant's attestation and approve eligibility.[15] To receive advance payment of the premium tax credit—during the inconsistency period and for the benefit year—an applicant must agree to file a tax return for the benefit year.[16] To receive advance payment of the premium tax credit during the

---

[10]PPACA, § 1411(e)(4)(A)(ii), 124 Stat. at 228; 45 C.F.R. § 155.315(f)(2).

[11]PPACA, § 1411(e)(3), 124 Stat. at 228; 45 C.F.R. § 155.315(b), (c), (f).

[12]PPACA, § 1411(e)(4), 124 Stat. at 228-229; 45 C.F.R. § 155.320(c)(3).

[13]PPACA, § 1411(e)(3)-(4), 124 Stat. at 228-229; 45 C.F.R. § 155.315(f)(4).

[14]PPACA authorizes the Department of Health and Human Services to extend the 90-day period for enrollments occurring during 2014. PPACA, § 1411(e)(4)(A)(ii), 124 Stat. at 228. CMS regulations also generally permit the marketplaces to extend the 90-day period if the applicant has made a good faith effort to obtain documentation required to resolve the inconsistency. 45 C.F.R. § 155.315(f)(3).

[15]45 C.F.R. § 155.315(g). This exception applies only to inconsistencies unrelated to citizenship or immigration status.

[16]45 C.F.R. § 155.310(d)(2)(ii)(A). If an individual who receives advance payment of the premium tax credit fails to file a federal income tax return for the benefit year, a marketplace is not permitted to approve eligibility for premium tax credits or cost-sharing reduction subsidies for the individual in a subsequent benefit year. 45 C.F.R. § 155.305(f)(4), (g)(1)(i)(B).

inconsistency period, an applicant also must attest to understanding that any advance payments of premium tax credits received during this period are subject to reconciliation.[17] Marketplaces are required to permit applicants to receive less than the full amount of advance payments of the premium tax credits in order to minimize the possibility of having to repay such credits if their actual income for the benefit year is higher.[18]

---

[17] 45 C.F.R. § 155.315(f)(4)(ii).

[18] 45 C.F.R. §155.310(d)(2)(i). Cost-sharing reductions are not subject to reconciliation on the taxpayer's federal income tax return.

www.ingramcontent.com/pod-product-compliance
Lightning Source LLC
Chambersburg PA
CBHW080807290526
45790CB00008B/3602